BILL
EVANS | MODERN
ADVENTURES

SPUYTEN DUYVIL

New York City

ACKNOWLEDGEMENTS

Thanks to the editors and staff of the following publications where many of
these poems first appeared:

"Back by Popular Demand," "Dear Penthouse," "Funk Machine," "How I Spent
my Summer Vacation," "Hubris was my Downfall," "Kiddie Porn," "Last of the
Wild Cupcakes," "Modern Adventures," "My Masterpiece," "Ode to Joan,"
"OK, Listen," "Opus," "The Playboy Advisor," and "Yo, Sappho" first appeared
in the exquisite cyber-zine *Exquisite Corpse* edited by Andrei Codrescu.

"Our Elvis" appeared in the anthology *Elvis Monologues* edited by Lavonne
Mueller, copyright 1998 Heinemann.

"What's Next" appeared in the anthology *Monologues from the Road* edited
by Lavonne Mueller, copyright 1999 Heinemann. The section on the letter X is
both indebted to and influenced by the chapter on the same letter from *Alpha
to Omega, The Life & Times of the Greek Alphabet* by Alexander and Nicholas
Humez, David R. Godine, Publisher, Boston, 1986.

"Epilogue," "Our Elvis," "Overture," and "Yo, Sappho" also appeared on the
spoken word CD *Collected Dark* by Bill Evans and Larry Dunn, Heat Warps
Records, copyright 2002 Bill Evans and Larry Dunn, distributed by Engine
Studios.

Thank you: Peter Catapano, Karen McWharter, Bez Ocko, Nava Renek,
Thaddeus Rutkowski, Joanna Sit, Michele Madigan Somerville, and
Tod Thilleman.

design: Karen McWharter and Bez Ocko
cover photograph: Karen McWharter
author photograph: Kristin McWharter

Library of Congress Cataloging-in-Publication Data

Evans, Bill (William Stephen), 1956-
  [Poems. Selections]
  Modern Adventures / Bill Evans.
     pages cm
  Poems.
  ISBN 978-0-923389-57-4
  I. Title.
  PS3605.V3643M63 2013
  811'.6--dc23

                    2013011018

"Endless unfolding of words of ages!
And mine a word of the modern, the word En-Masse."

Walt Whitman, *Song of Myself*

"I was me again…
The sky was vast. The night was clear.
I felt on the brink of a grand adventure.
What could it be?"

Maira Kalman, *Max in Hollywood, Baby*

for the Xtra Virgins

MODERN ADVENTURES

LAST OF THE WILD CUPCAKES

WHAT'S NEXT

MODERN
ADVENTURES

OK, LISTEN

The job is killing
Me, no
Being me
Or me
Being you
Who will
Play us
In the movie?
Dot to dot
Molecules
Tongue and
Groove souls
Being famous
Some star
Taking his or
Her shirt off
But is it art
And who cares
O wily audience?
I mean, you do
We do, being
Caring people
Half dead, half
Deadly, but the
Other half alive!
And that's the half
I am addressing at
This present moment
Don't go away; we'll be
Right back! Right after
This word from our
Commercial sponsor...

I shall now sing
A song – O
Run like hell
The future is
Out there, a
Giant television

Fashion orders
From the Gap
Everybody in
Pilgrim clothes
Everybody naked
Pressed between
Pages – damn, I
Always meant to
Write that book first

And I ask you, what
Happened? What
Shoot me, *occurred?*

Anyway, we missed it
Being painfully occupied
Always wooing when we
Should've been thinking
Always thinking when we
Should've been wooing
Or thinking about wooing
Or not thinking, woo-less
Un-wooable, de-wooified

Everybody
In prison
Clothes
Antarctic
Swimwear
Everybody
In cans
Dreaming
Robot dreams

Our donut
Theory of
Radical
Accomplishment

"Is it a circle
Or a zero?"
"Mine's got
Sprinkles!"
"My what big
Teeth you have
Granny!" "Oh, really..."

Children
We are
Stories
And we
Do not last
Deep luck
And mystery
Energy, get over it

You only know
Where you
Can go
Those
You don't
Choose, choose you

And I love best
What loves me
Opening at theaters soon, then closing

Sincerely, you can quote that

DEAR PENTHOUSE

I always thought your letters were fake, but
Recently I had an experience...
Dear Penthouse
What is love?
Can a modern guy
Find authentic happiness
While pursuing
An authentically
Modern career, say
Talking on a cell phone
To authentic chicks
I like your magazine
Because the sex
Is, well, dirtier
And I actually live
In a penthouse apartment!
And the thing is
You have taste
Hot articles and stuff
Sometimes I even think I
Might major in journalism
Dear Penthouse, what is realism?
Hardon hard-hitting, go-go go-getting

The entire textual world eroticized

A gesture of naked Penthousian enthusiasm

Cute fans
Unzipping
My typewriter

As I write these words

Adieu to loneliness

Beats the pants off your MBA
Your MFA, hell, college, drugs

Predictable as
Weather
In her
Dress of
Many seasons

Unpredictable as
Weather
With her
Yes of
Many reasons

Nude as truth
On an icy plate
Beneath the porn
Stars in the sky
Beaming interstellar energies

Arousing us to action
From our complicated slumber

Into lusty vignette –

As a freshman
At a large
Prestigious
University

Imagine my surprise when/
Peeking through
A hole through/
Great beauties whose
Wit and rue I bore/
As well as fluffy towels
And squirt-bottles of conditioner/

For my joy was to serve
As virginal as spring
O crispish autumn, fiery thunder-spore
Icing winter with his wild tongue
All varieties of wicked and collected grief
No more grief, I say an *end* to *grief*
Great mischief or intrigue as residential antidote
We need a language made of that

They were the girls next door
On another planet
And I, their humble trainee
Equipment-boy space-man

Though to Salome and Kansas I was always "Torpedo"

And that's when things turned plain interesting

SOMETHING NEW

Always "in search of"
Rarely "content"
The idea being
This, *now*
Which occurs
Through time
And includes
Fucking everything
While appearing
Neatly singular
And wildly
Instantaneous
As if it truly were
Just me speaking
Secretly to you
Instead of building a bridge

Which it is, I mean
The bridge part, as
In "built" or "made"
I would say more
Recognized than
Artfully constructed
And it's a public bridge
Crossed together by events
Jammed with public talk
Slightly glamorous and
Artificial, on one hand, if
You must – yet going someplace real

And as for secrets, well, actually
There aren't any
The world is there
You're here
Little pilgrim, we're so
Proud of you
Straight shooter, serious reader
Spelunker after facts
Deep diver into myth
And public text, masterful swimmer
Of municipal waterways/
Absolutely modern as all get out
Fashionably equipped, devilishly stylish –

X-ray goggles, see through clothes!

Techno-literate in form, soulful, tuneful...

Brethren, each landscape
Covets attitude
Some bridges span eons
Seeking only
To connect
Fate waits
Choice chooses
As if luck would have us
Positively warped
And wooed by our journeys
Weather will not stop us
Rain and snow shall fail to deny
Our glorious arrivals, just like the post office

So believe me, bridge
Be a finger
Pointing
And rage on
O bridge builders
I mean build on, shine

We give the finger
To time, kids
Loss and
Her cousins
For every word spells
Goodbye and
Great movement apes waving

We didn't do it
For the money
I'll say that much

Next, we would be better
And last longer

Don't get stuck on the bridge

KIDDIE PORN

Use would be
Made of
Footage of
Candy

Mounds
Of it, gobs
Himalayas
Whole Alps

Later, after
Gameboy
Bangs
Barbie

Bubble gum

Cigars
In the
Pepsi
Jacuzzi

Marshmallow

Stars

Fiery four-

Leaf clovers, chocolate hearts

NAKED PICTURES OF FAVORITE TEACHERS

Much is best left
Unknown, though
I have them, if
You want them –

Big talkers with
Official bellies
Gaga articulate
As primal forms

Some impersonate
Cavemen, whereas
Others graph equations

The really hot ones
Are frequently blurred

From impressive thought
A molecular occurrence

Product organized
By subject area
And century
Of origin

Viewer XX
Discretion
Categorically
Advised

Side effects include
Blindness
Left-handedness
Telepathy
Promiscuity
Precognition
Postcognition
Echolocation
Electrocution
And/or cold fusion

Transformation
Into stone is rare
Though reports vary

But why worry
Horrible things
Happen to everyone
Vegetarians eaten by wolves
Safes falling out of the sky and conking monks

Kids, you grow up
You fall *in love*
You even get
To do it / here
And there / there
And here, hell, wherever

Hey, plane goes down
In Arctic or Amazon
You'll be spanking glad to have
Purchased these Polaroids

More dependable, more durable
Than laptop computers –
Scientifically proven to
Ward off vampires!
Relax and shoo
Monsters all
Snuggy
In your
Sleepy bags

As you wait to be
Educated
Wait to
Be saved
Maybe even
Rescued
Recovered
Discovered
Claimed
Reclaimed
As they say
Transposed
Not to mention
Recognized
Found, found out
Excuse me, declassified
Demystified, transmogrified
Blah blah blah, till you're woozy with pedagogy

Say bye-bye, Bigfoot

Night-night, snake

And then the dream guys arrive
In their four wheel drives

Bearing fabulous certificates
And cash prizes

Of poetry and algebra...

And in the morning
It'll all be better
Or else broken
Differently
Uses galore
An erotic
Krazy glue
To hold the
Pieces back together

Not answers, questions
Mindful lumps
Little heart-shaped blobs
Secret scars, tattoos
All proofs of an amazing
And authentic humanity –

Visa and Mastercard
Readily accepted
IOU's against
Future allowances
Eagerly invested
In spirit bank accounts

Yes, on winged steeds
With chubby butts
You can own
These images
A bit heavy
On the artifice
But the point is
When you need us
Gosh, we're there!
And the point is
When you don't
Heck, we're still there!

At the bottom
Of the
Backpack
Mixed
Up, deep –

Suitable for framing
And sizable erasure
Cheap, but never easy
Accessible, available

AND NOW FOR THE WISDOM PORTION OF OUR PROGRAM

Counselor Troy has regained consciousness!
I paid for it in blood
Despair *is* a kind of song
Poet would be fine
The world needs one
We saddled up our cantos
And lit the hell out –
Theoretically erotic
As well as available

I will get around to the
Important part later
We searched
Our souls
There was
Nothing there!
Resign into the flow
Please, take off
Your clothes
Look, look, the bridges are melting

Aim carefully; I'm in here

You only log 60
Billion miles once
I will keep this brief
What a revelation

Would that be
The real real
Or the fake real
Just kidding...

And of course
To seek, but
Do not find
Or else to find

And forget to seek!

Or you might
Go to sleep
And I could
Kiss your ear

But till then you
Can bite me

ODE TO JOAN

for Leelee Sobieski

Not being a vision
Doubter myself, I
Also have been chosen
To command misfits

Drive the English
Out of France
Drive the English
Department
Out of wrecking poetry!

Transform serious
Loser energy
Into fearsome love

Or whatever, O
Leelee of Arc
In Times Square –

Big movie-star head
And a suit of armor
Tall girl, in heels
According to Selena

O we have seen miracles
On our TV's, but I didn't
Watch all of it; I watched
Some of it: evil bad guys

Humble village folk, loyal
Blind kid, skanky dauphin
Peter O'Toole as the rotten
Representative of a corrupt

And powerful religious oligarchy
O damn them all Leelee, excuse me, Joan
Fierce teenage kick-ass virgin warrior
Whose heart was so pure it refused to burn

And died, can you believe it, forgiving *everyone*

But not me, like history, I keep grudges
And as an artist, I plot revenge
The nourishing of scars, the
Nurturing of petty and vindictive swipes

A heart so positively flammable
Ouch, it carries warning labels

(Deep tequila charged with dark vanilla –)
(Packs a wallop and then some –)

Listen, I am not a saint
And there is no God
But if there were
As statistically
Improbable as
His or her taking
Any kind of interest
In French politics…

For the record
Praise wild
Belief; praise
Hacking off
One's hair
And wearing
Roguish clothes
Praise risk; praise
Bearing one's standard
Praise the very record
And the preposition "for"

For joyous are the mysteries
Brought to us by television

For the flames
Were real

And the feet
Were hers

The people
Needed her

THE PLAYBOY ADVISOR

As Playboy guys
We try to keep in mind
The Playboy philosophy
Hey, let's call room service

As hepcats of articles
And stunning pictorials
We honor the rituals
Suave urban in principle

Lounge around the manse
In our Playboy pajamas
We're never going out
If we can delve within!

Hmm, an interview
With Kevin Kline
New babe on Baywatch
The *real* J. Peterman

Our college-educated
Stewardess girlfriends
Are Playboy women
Athletic and liberated

Who enjoy fine art
And arrive each month
Flush with fashion, fiction
Candid conversation

Official Playboy
Rabbit-head key chain
Reminding us of
Easter and epic transformation

Also, thank you, St. Claus as erotic sprite
While the kiddies are nestled
All snug in their waterbeds
Guess who's doing it with Playboy mom

'Cause it's a Playboy world
And everybody gets some
A vision of the naughty
And the nice as one

Plus a fancy pad
Stocked with
Shocking treats, O
Naked as our tousled mammal hearts! Mad civilized, jacuzzied…

ODE TO A PAIR OF PANTS

I look down and you're gone!
OK, I can do this
There are worse faux pas
Whole lists of more
Grievous and mortal terrors
My life, for example
And that's just
The first example
Look, everyone dreams
But a clown wakes
And wearing underwear
Juggles roaring chainsaws...
Still, it's rather chilling
Reading poems without you
Spanking funny how the audience
Doesn't laugh/ they have no idea

ODE TO MY SHOES

Shoes, you are
There, and
That says
A lot of it

I count
More
Of you
Than I
Have feet

Which is
A measure
Of success

And stately
Diplomatic
Progress

O

Boots
Sandals
Flippers
Espadrilles
Mukluks
Slipper-
Socks

Brogans...

Long, long
Were the
Reckless
Nights
And the
Reckless days

Driving cranky sheep

But a barefoot waif
Amongst toothsome wolves
Far from the Sorbonne
And a degree in Theology

God's lights in the sky an illuminated map

And a dream of walking the high wire

Through Paris, in springtime, metaphysical and sheepless

Thus, it would be by luck
Plus the miracle of grace
That I might salvage
What remained of
Shy fledgling nobility
And through the service
Of an expert and divine
Concentration, rediscover

My way

Anyway
That was
The plan

Subtract
A few
Eons for
Pining
And yearning

The lost
Years
The punk
Years
The drunk
Out of
My mind
Years, the
Vaguely
Fuzzy years
The claiming
A career years
The harnessed to
The combine years
The pirate years
The spaceship years

Three-card monte years

Playboy / cowboy years

The years of sleight of hand
And look before you leap
The years of waking up
And now I fake me down to sleep

The *excruciating* surfer years, Jesus!
Talk about swimming/cursing/paddling
The years busting my beatnik, hepcat ass
Just to capture one genius, avenger wave

And then the Zen years
Man, riding that
Baby *everywhere!*

I mean way-out, people...

And through each
Of these adventures
I wore shoes
Except for the
Surfing part
There I wore
Foot soles
And a tiny
Professional
Bikini-bottom
Bathing suit
All the better to merge
With the predominate
Compound that designates this planet
In a natural and scenic ecological habitat
Look snappy and Tarzanic in the postcard/photographs

Which I hereby bequeath to my
Authorized biographers

Come what may

But, attention!
Brother shoes
Whom I swear I

Shall keep

Unless my dingbat heirs

Try to sell you at a flea market –

Because by then
I'll be dead
And off
Tending
Sheep again

Navigating my tribe of itsy, kung fu lamby-pies

Through the grand constellations in a burning rowboat

And sadly
You guys
Will be left
On your own
You'll be all alone
At the mercy of commerce

It makes me *cringe*
To think of life
As a commodity

We all know Hell
Is full of lawyers
And tattooists
And I am damned
If I'm not happy here
Pierced and illustrated
While screwing celebrities
Penning poetry to porn stars
Cable-magic TV and pop chat sites
Pokémon, Teletubbies, Baywatch
Barney, Ben Franklin, Tomboy Jefferson
Don't forget the Marilyns: Monroe *and* Manson

Authoring my suit
Drawing up
My suit
Endlessly
Revising
Tantalizing
Details, shaving
Evidence, clarifying

Arguments/
Pleading
Presenting
Espousing

Representing

In the name
Of fairness
And justice
And the rest
In the name of yes

In the name of you bet

In the spirit of
The lost lost
And the found lost
And the lost again

Pardon me, I digress
Your honors
Various in majesty

BACK BY POPULAR DEMAND

I can count on one finger
The reasons
For being here
Bouncy and fit
Flush with outer
Space and a deck
Smack with aces
Ethernet surfboard
Troubadour tattoo
Slung saddlebag
Of pirate songs
Leaping from my power chord

Quarters in
The meter
Darling, all

For you/

Any wild heart
With a half-life
Long enough

Any jet-pack knapsack
Of slacker awe
Stone ready to commence
The elected transformation

Because we used
To be lost, now
We're found
"Amazing Grace"
Great ditty by
A slave trader
We used to be
Reflection
Now we're ACTION

Get your whites
Whiter, your
Brights brighter

Farewell
Fond nights
In detention/exile

Memorizing classics
While handcuffed to the bed post

Practicing my smile
As righteous snoozers
Euphemistically butchered innocent poetry

I have checked
With my parole board
And know this to be true

Besides, we got the ruby slippers

Whatever…

And of course
Through woe
Your invitation
Woke me and
For that I am
Grateful/
Genius
Scrub-faced
Apple-bottomed
Serving girl from
Anyplace, PA –

Who I also can be

With renegade integrity

For mighty are the signs

MODERN ADVENTURES

To begin at the end
And move backwards
Sweet battery
Of knockout
Burnout energy
Lookin' like a hero
In a textbook mirror
With the strength of Ra!

All the way
From out there
To in here
I'm betting everything
On everything, always, alas

It is, and
It isn't
It should be
But won't
The glass
Half naked
Or half clothed
That's something

For what is important
Is rarely
Comforting
Both speaker
And receiver
A collage of masks
O flatterers of massive
Anxiety and sex appeal

Suddenly, I
Ask for shit
And I get it

Go figure...

So one becomes
The instrument
Etc. And so forth
"Patricia, I was stoned!"
As virginal as spring
Another loser king
At the seasonal roulette table

I don't know
Rock star
Performance artist

Blur of dreamy hair
Across a neon heart, whatever

But will it play
On Mars?
A far cry –
Check your
Basket of kisses
For prize upon entering

The very symbols
You are wearing
Suit you perfectly

Sure, a lot is fake
We'll want
Those, too!
Believe it if
You must, or
Because *you do*

Oh yeah, and
Another thing

Not searching, finding

The great sap rising
From our fiery
Technology

We don't need
Further training
We need passion, vision

I stand by my philosophy

LAST OF
THE WILD CUPCAKES

HOW I SPENT MY SUMMER VACATION

In a suit of armor
On a nude beach
Beneath a flag:
Burning pants
On a mop handle –
Surfboard, long
Sword and trusty
Badminton racket, ho!
Beside a pile of torn-luck Lotto cards
Sleeping in the car
And eating air
Deciphering the, editing the... omens

Which got me here
I'd like to start there
Very happy to arrive
Either whole or in pieces

Positively ravishing
Tonight, dear scars
Let us utilize this moment
To notice everyone

Now we'll listen to the messages
Found on my machine

Is this Bill Evans the musician?
Bill Evans the weatherman?
Bill Evans the actor?
Bill Evans the stockbroker?
Bill Evans the publicist?
Bill Evans the broncobuster?
Bill Evans the philanthropist?
Bill Evans the producer of "Cats"?

Oh, take a little trip
Tour scenic Hell
You'll thrill to the descent
Plus the long, artful
Schlep back home
Break a billion rules
Sneak forbidden peeks
Duke it out with loss, metaphorically speaking
Loser, you too
Can be a famous poet
Proud owner of the tooth
That pierces the heart
And the mouth that sings

HUBRIS WAS MY DOWNFALL

I never meant to kill my father or
Marry my mother or
Tear out my eyes and
Become a kind of mangy
Seer wandering around
What was it, Crete or ancient Greece?
Anyway, Colonus, where the hell
Is that? I mean, it wasn't
In the plan, if I even
Had one. Who me, king?
Well, fuck you too
"Temper, temper." Yeah. Right

And as far as that flying too close
To the sun stuff
Crappy technology
Did me in. Not a bad
Bad flight as bad flights go
Once again, I didn't listen
Yuck! Feathers, blobs of
Wax! Kind of goopy
But exciting, even *exhilarating*
The necessary plummet
Was a bit much. I believe I learned something

However, my supreme *coup de grâce*
Was the creation of life
From used body parts
An eclectic synthesis of
Interests and careers spanning
Years in med school, engineering, a short stint as a neighborhood
      grave robber
Several high school summers at the recycling plant...
I truly feel that of all my failures
This one particular brave example
Speaks volumes for those clever human
Qualities that make me unique
Everyone dreams of giving the finger
To fate and death, blind witless authorities
Ladies and gentlemen, I am that finger. I'm pointing the way

LAST OF THE WILD CUPCAKES

Arise, arise, you worthless fuckers
And get with it!
I've walked away
From more than this

Thankful
I am not
That one

Many wished for wishes
And thought
Themselves clever

Our platform
Is various
And uniquely satisfying

If elected, I refuse to serve

All applications must be
Danced in person

The toady mentality
Is currently
"A rage"

Whose butt
Do I kiss towards
What stellar mediocrity?

Our serious career of
Being a sled dog
Has drawn to a
Subtle and tragic close

No longer mentoring
Future
Golf
Enthusiasts/

Wake me when
It's over
Or started, whatever...

You who are poets, imagine
A good one
Kind of dumb
But cute. Points for trying

You're not
A joker
You're a player
Be back
In a
Minute

You can't even step
In the same
River once!

Now that poetry
Is chic
Umm
What
About
Results?

Our product
Exists. You can
Thank us for that

So you won't be saved
But you may grow
Amused

Besides

Clean up
Is a
Chore or snap

To woo. To cook. To make maps

And naturally –

A big fish
In a small pond
Or a small fish
In a big pond, or a GIANT
Fish in a COLOSSAL pond, or
No fish, no pond, just
Fishness, pondness: two principles

It's morphin'
Time. Power Up
We may be
Fast
But
We're
Never easy

Very risky
To think

"Yeah, loss *should* sing…"

Hold a grudge?
You bet
Revenge? Why
Certainly!

Another
Genius
Reason
To have
Suffered so
Effectively

The real weapon

Is the King's English

OUR ELVIS

Fat mechanic with thick sideburns
And carefully combed back, jump-back hair
Satin kind of pajama suit
Rhinestoney as a galaxy! Here in this
Funky country bar where we have
Escaped, O rockabilly hideaway!
Saturday, late, while the last
Paycheck dances. And you city folk think
Rednecks don't know how to swing

This afternoon, this guy, he
Fixed my car. And tonight
Tonight, he's a fucking star!
Light-years more living
Than the original
He's a fake
But who isn't?

I never got to see the real one
The famous one
The King
One, the dead one, the
Kidnapped by
Aliens one
The pill-
Head one
The one who roams
The stellar
Mojo incognito
The one I read about
Breathlessly in
Supermarket checkout lines
Recorder of my favorite spaced-out Christmas tune:

Merry Christmas, baby/
You sure do treat me right, etc.
Bought me a diamond ring for Christmas/
Now I'm livin' in Paradise, etc.

White Negro
Mama's boy
Blues thief
Graceland
Immortal
Rock and Roll
Icon demigod
Cracker heartthrob
With a taste for
Jailbait and a *voice*

Whose effective persona
Focused public attention
On the physical arena
Of hot teenage sexuality

Quite a threat to authority
And patriarchal masculinity
Masked as musical commodity
Stressing action and relation

I mean the subtext of
DOING IT
Versus
OWNING IT
A very dangerous
Addition to bourgeois pop culture
From the war
Rooms of the poor

And shit, *that* Elvis
Wouldn't touch my car
We'd still be stuck
In the rain
Afar...
Full electrical
Spark plug
Burn out/
Pottstown
Pennsylvania
1990 something –
Kiwi Shoe Polish
Mrs. Smith's Pies
Former methamphetamine capital
Of the Eastern Seaboard
There to visit grandma
And grandpa McWharter
Very near the end of our century, the Twentieth
North American international
Info-technological
Televisional metaphysical Christian evangelical
Theoretical magical financial empire, U. S. of A.

Where I, umm
Reside and
Reluctantly travel

Culture Warrior
School of
Realistic
Anecdotalism

Offer my
Report
Another
Bigmouth try

And wave
A giant
Anecdotal
Cult-War "hi"
To his highness
Clyde "Little Elvis" Monroe

Of Monroe and Monroe

Towing and Repair –

Hero of
This poem
Right
Now and forever

Blasting
His secular
Self mic-ward

Elder brother
To Ezekiel
Monroe on
Saxophone

The fabulous Monroe
Sisters
Gina
And
Angela

Assorted
Cousin
Monroes
Bashing
Various
Percussives

And, golly, dear
Audience

And heck
Everybody!

Whose *Heartbreak Hotel*
Is a
Radical
Miracle

I'm telling you

OVERTURE

Attention, this is the life
You bet your butt on
Before the court of
Your own startled
Adolescence
A small fame
Actually, but
Vivid and exact
I mean, "You rip, dude!"
Graceful, graceless
With compassionate abandon

And this is the way
We go to school
Tie our shoes
Practice curses or caresses
Join the bigmouth squad and shoot these words
At the assembled heads
Stately mayhem tattoos across the best and worst of us
I mean why not now and
What's in it for me?
It was a wrestling match because beauty
Isn't truth nor truth beauty

And this is what I've learned
From studying poetry:
Suplex, High Crotch, Crab Ride
Double Grape Vine, Take Down
*Near Fall, Pin...*We only write them
To win, of course, but loss
Remains increasingly useful
And strategically accurate.You don't
Just kick ass; you also make points. Points
Then ass, ass then points. That's the duty of our team endeavor/
Transformation, redistribution, Hell, redemption, a very secular
     salvation, a new fucking honesty

OPUS

The contest is not popularity
I forget what I
Said next
And now
We are back
Off with
Their heads!
Become a good boy –
Richer
More stable

Oh, flattery
Will get you
Kansas City
Dignify experience
Then complain
Play hard ball
In the big leagues
With the real heavies
The fashionable vanguard
Of our telling personalities/

O flesh made Word...

To divide by zero
And not be imaginary
She was the love
Of my life
She had snakes
Instead of hair
Special thanks to the horizon
For staying so unreachable
They took away my
Pirate ship
That hurt too!
Will you kiss
A hand? Will you
Lick a boot?
Came to recognize a hot
Sound when we blew one
If it doesn't
Kill you, you're doin' OK

And grow, if not wise, at least
Arrogant and witty. Give the guy
His award. Throw in a TV
Why, we could go anywhere
Believing in our everything!
As if a beautiful language
Were spanking a tree, don't
Listen to THEM; listen TO ME

You've been bashed
Around, but
I think you're great
Will you pose
Naked while I
Write these poems?

Build a temple
In my mouth
For a racy goddess

(Don't get yr crowns
Mixed up with
Yr thrones!)

May we dream
In tongues

CRIMES AGAINST THE LIBRARY

Fucking in the stacks
Certainly. Eating
Or being eaten
Blow jobs, rim jobs
Hand jobs. Snarling
Like a wild man. Drooling
Foaming, creaming
Stalking. Making others
Uncomfortable
Challenging the aura
Of scholarly aplomb
Of course, burning books
Igniting one's clothing
Hair, small campfires
Speaking rudely
To one's servants
Spanking one's servants
Tethering a horse
Retiring an ass. The singing of
Folk songs or sea chanteys
The construction of a vessel
On instructions from God

Farming, especially tobacco
The building of cities
And draining of swamps
Excess use of slave labor
Disingenuous space travel
Excess use of the whip
Excess use of the cross
Excess of tears and
The gnashing of teeth
False love. Phony sincerity
Excess of drunkenness
And sobriety. Cheapness
Of tip. Smallness of vision
Also hubris, idolatry, adultery
Frivolity, eschatology, archery and tennis

Need I mention the importance
Of pure thought?
Remember, we're watching
Listening, reading, filing
Feeling anything
You feel, first
Deciding on the order
Filling in the facts
We're not selling
We're lending. You have
To give it back
You get to take it home
But you have to return
Out and back, back
And out. The books are
Just a shill; they don't
Mean shit. The connection
The movement means everything

YO, SAPPHO

Much would be decided in passing
For example, who did what
To whom
And even where
And why, sometimes
And what of it

The temple all
A shambles/
The temple left
In tatters/

Either dawn or dusk
Well, that's
One approach

Sing in me
Muse
I mean
Rock on
Sisters...

Memory's kids
With their alternative

Mentality/ O
Hot, slow
Hard, strong
Sound be
With us
And guide us

Go out
And
Return
Push away
And come back

Talk about a
Kind of emptiness
As the glory
Of our culture

Been there
Done that
Is anyone awake?

Impossible, therefore
Sign us up!
Remember us as symbols, signals

Flags where there is no wind, but waving anyway

IN THE THROES OF HABITAT

Up yours
Spring
Gash open
My heart
For love's sake

Thanks for
The exploding
Valentine

Funny
You should
Mention everything

Busy learning
Not to
Curse
Or even
Think
Too
Much

After all
I am a
Role model

Praise
Yes
Exult
Okay

Smoke
A gum
Cigar with
Aaron and Haldo

But don't tell their moms

Because you rock
That's our
Comedy secret

Because why
Not now and
What's in it for me?

Because we
Are your leaders
These are orders

Have poems
Will travel, just
Never leave the house

Absolutely modern
With stylish technology
– Surfboards, tattoos, piercings, tags, gels, zest, gusto,
        muscles, allure

And of course
Music full
Whammo
Hip-hop city
On an island hill

Where we live and breathe
True instruments of culture
Down with Coltrane, Miles, Buffy *and* Chaucer

Learn to cook
And slay, slay
And cook

Tastes good
Sounds
Great
Looks
Hot
Fine
Be that
Be mine

FUNK MACHINE

Hold on to this for a minute
Make mine
To go
Act IV
Scene 2
Where they
Throw the poet
Into the volcano

Behind him
His twelve
Scantily
Garbed and
Dancing wives
Sing background vocals

Everywhere
Children
And iced
Pineapple
Silver machetes

         Drugs, *and worse*!

The visiting missionaries shiver, aghast
The local deities

         Will be fed!

Once again, peace
Shall reign
In the kingdom

       Pumpkin carriages
       Winged watermelons
       Traditional penis thongs…

And yes, it's a far
Cry from Cleveland
Stalwart kids
Wee lassies
And buckoes
You gotta read
A lotta books
Meet a lot of
Saintly, dignified
Presbyterian ministers in
Lady Putt-Putt's pleasure garage
Swab a lot of decks on the Captain's
Pirate barge, play hooky, snooker, eat vitamins, salad, haul
Toboggans, chop down rain forests, learn to talk snake –

And when you come out
The other side
If in fact
You survive
To the other
Side, it's a
Brand new hemisphere

(Holy gosh-
Darn Toledo!)

Constellations and everything

Those who make it
Are amazed
And live
Upside
Down
Their
Feelings
Reversed
Into positive
Constructions

Sadness as
Joy, fear
As strength
Shame as
Compassion
Hopelessness
As faith and so
On and so forth; you get
The picture. Elaborate visuals
We can set aside. Excess logic has an overrated place
Let's forget that too

Because right now, it's just me
And you. And what I say
Goes, though very quickly
Yo, a moment. Humor me
OK? I don't waste
A thought. I can tell
You are a smart audience
Laughter and dashing sexuality
I sense, in the best sense
Leaking from the lot of you

So, imagine/
In the movie
We can play
Ourselves

We are
The stars

We sport
Charming
Astrologies

And though the meaning may be strange
The film is
Damnably impressive

Amend to our names
The phrase *prize-winning*
Brothers and sisters

LANGUAGE LESSON

Jackson says, "Can I say
Jeez-o-man?" I think
For a minute imagining
Teachers, grandmothers, honest
Ordinary citizens, all the so-called
Adult type, authority type, would-be word
Police vocabulary monitors my kid will be
Dealing with now that he's officially
Growing up and in Pre-K school

"Yeah, you can say
Jeez-o-man," I say
Daddy-savvy

Jackson says
"Jeez-o-man,
Jeez-o-man,
Jeez-o-man…"

"But Dad, I can't say fuckin'."

"Right, you can't say fuckin'."

"Can I say grasshopper?"

"You can say grasshopper."

Jackson says, "But not fuckin' grasshopper. Right, Dad?"

MY MASTERPIECE

Of course, I was somewhere else
As the glorious event
Was just getting started
Don't mind me, I thought
Washing out the coffee pot
A little scrub-magic kitchen
Commando Sufi dance
Whirling contentedly through
Spot-remover laundry mode
I am absolutely nothing
If I am not thorough
After various risqué
And modern adventures
I like an ordered home

Because home is where you hang
Your hat, where the hats
Hang their heads, where the heart is
Hung on the family
Meat rack, hang out
With your friends, that is
If you have any –
The pistols locked tastefully
In their decorative display case
Beneath the mounted noggins of our personable forbears

So I will take the world
Thanks, with sauce
Tape a naked Iceland to an
Available sarcophagus
Surf the big waves
With the big dogs
For the big thoughts
Big *(not!)* Big feeling in the details
Of our mystical estrangement
Big shot, big fuss, big mess, big bridge, big buildings, big
     orphic cubism

Big *New York City* to you, fiery pilgrim

Big mouth, big plans, big deal

THE CIVILIZING ELEMENT

Yeah, well, many
Were the joyous
Discoveries, people
And many damn fine
Hearts did serve
And many didn't
Make it, many
Hands snapped off
As they rose to splurge
All over those elected
Volunteer yeses
Many typewriter
Accidents and
Crashed saxophones
Drunks and nuts
To the deluxe-
Boxed ones of us
The famous poet
Rolling his eyes
As I slammed through
The names from our
Dismembered past – still
They were the language
Animals that raised me
And I owe them big time

Then I walked across the room
To check out Jessie and
In blew Mia, flush
With her new
Life in a new
Apartment
Jessie really
Pissed from
A hallway dis –
I mean, *who*
Does the *guy*
Think he *is*?
Professorial moms
Distributing wine
And little cheese-
Puff quiche nabs
To the assembled masses
And no one even got loaded
Or smashed any furniture
And all the clothes were kept on

And later in the cab on the way with the girls, I
Sat between them for luck
As our pumpkin transported us
Westward ho, across the magic city
And fortunately, Jessie knew the address
Because we were on the guest list, and Lyla said
That the glorious event simply could not commence until
    we three arrived

ROGUE SOUND

Personally, I don't
Believe things get
Better the further
Back you go wham
Into some golden
Age of fleecy
Sentiment everybody
Work work work lovey
Dovey for the man or
King big honky
Fella in a line top
Down as in Shakespeare
The immortal bard
Bald head quill pen
Sung by English
Departments everywhere

And I don't believe in
Nature either shark
Eat newt newt eat frog
Hog molecules thrashing
Around through primal soup
Atoms smashing the
Shit out of other atoms
Have some gravity
Don't mind if I do
Sit on the damn eggs
Read Darwin and evolve
Build cities dream culture
Wow, it's so dark
And like really scary
Care to look at my cave paintings?

And only a fool
Believes in technology
Maybe the bicycle gun or
Long bow but TV sucks and
Computers are basically filing cabinets
Whacked on speed like my
Whole generation before AA
NA and various rehabs
Altered the face of
Glamorous addiction
You would not believe
How many celebrities
Turn to coffee and God
As their drug of choice

But I don't believe in God
How can I? I just believe
In me. Yoko and me. And that's reality

EPILOGUE

Yes, you would need to be there
A hunter/gatherer
Type of affair

Dread has worn
These boots
A demanding
Explanation!

Dreaming mostly of
Removing her
Whatevers

Salary commensurate with
Lotto fever

We don't believe
In God, so we
Don't need goals

Not exactly
The atom
Bomb of
Ripstop
Careerism

Our values are
Get us
Outta here!

You know, empires
Come and go, but
The weather *arrives*

Tennis, anyone?

And I release thee, trapped spirit. Thou hast done
Thy job passably

What doesn't suck?
We sail
At dawn. The swords are drawn

WHAT'S NEXT

WHAT'S NEXT

Sorry about the
Rotten ending
You either get
Used to things
Or you don't
Another teenage
Heart forgotten
At the salad bar
Make the world
A better place for
Troubadour poetics
Zorro is our man
At the end of long
Alphabets
Who will tell you that it sucks
Being chosen, so choose
Like, choose your mask
Choose cunning and revenge
Choose absolutely devastating, stylish swordplay
The hacienda is lonely tonight, little flower
The rest of us have gone off to taunt rich priests and piss
       sweetly in the sea

Because we would be heroes
Of epic
Whatevers –
Romantic in
The best sense
With irony
And claws
That our cause
Would be because
Our stated mission
Inadmissible
We'll have lots of
Explaining to do
In the morning, but
Heroes are friendly
And thrive on chat
A useful quality to practice
While yearning endlessly
I'm working on it

Listen, I will be
The moon
And sing to you
In Spanish
Or you will sing
And I'll be me
Oh, just take off your clothes

We don't have time
For fake gestures
We can barely touch
What we are *now*
And I am in exile
From my kingdom
Grieve with me nakedly
Spirit-fed poet girl
I will bring you donuts
And loose electrons
Even hook you up to an
Illegal cable box – Darling
Think of it, millions
Of channels! You can use
My electric toothbrush!
Such intimate aggression
Doesn't come cheap
Vitamin E oil, vitamin C
Say, fifty-dollar bills
As our minimum currency

Because real shit is happening
Please hold
My calls
We must
On The Road
Ourselves
Into their anthology

Wow!

Some
Road!

And here
We
Are
On it

O

Hipsters
Roadsters
Zen masters
Poetasters

Perhaps a slice a pie
Or a pinch o dope

"Jack Kerouac wore khakis"
And so on...

Let me tell you
'Bout our car
Trip to Neverland –

Afro-Cubop
In form, cheeseburger
Fries and giant
Shake plus
Toy a la Walt
Disney
Toxic
Plastic
Chinese
Warrior
Made in China
Actually
Karate chops
Fruit of new
Global movie
Economy
Multi-
Cultural
But only vaguely nutritional

Also somewhat collectable

This just in

From division of
Pop
Investment, comrade accountants
Many roads
And skills
But one map
Inked by olden
Pirates
Secretive of treasure

X for Christ
For the cross
For crossbones

X for a kiss
For the signature
Of the illiterate

X marks the spot
An algebraic unknown

X for the
Saxophone
X for sex

X-crossed fingers as a prayer for luck
For absolution from the punishments of lying

Walt's frozen you know
Packed on ice
At the rocket
Control panel
Of a company
Space ship in
Disney headquarters/

Mouseketeer, Florida

He left detailed instructions

First they're gonna thaw Walt out
Then they're gonna fix
What's wrong
I guess death –
They're gonna fix
Walt's death
(He's got all
Kinds of talented
Brainiacs on retainer)

Walt shall sip
From a
Mug of joe

Walt shall
Smoketh
A reentry Marlboro

Walt shall check
His email; Walt shall pee

Friendly shake to reactivated thank you Disney wiener

Then smack back
To work
A defrosted
American
CEO visionary
Pause for ignition, animation, lift off, millennial empire, juicy
    plunder, Oscar
Emmy, Tony, Obie
Not to mention syndication
And product licensing
Unlike us, unlike me
Slowpoke
Lazy-
Bones
Complainer
Beat Generation wanna be

Impossible, surly employee

So done I'm gone, like a wild door closing

Write your own line here

Out the window
There are trees
Bushes really

Dizzy Gillespie
And his
Orchestra
On tape deck
Ladies and gentlemen

We're only going 70
That's not speeding

Jackson
Explaining
Today's
Dream

Several talking
Fish fishing
For fishermen...

That the poem
Gets *made*
Instead of
Felt or *said*
Transmissions
From an outside
To a user self
In any language that remains
Oh, fuck me
Available

Dig there, pilgrim

And the shake
Is good too
Chocolate
Slight
Malt
No milk
Or milk
Products
No ice cream
Not even shook
More like dispensed
Yes, stirred or mixed then artfully dispensed

Through a robotic urn

Because we
Like our
Vices
Socially
Dependable

Neon motel
Chambermaid
With nipple ring
And lace –

And that's so nice
The road can be
So messy

Catch you later
In the mirror
If I can get
Away with it

I got pools

To sail

Kids

To swim

Laps to praise

Bill Evans was born in Forty Fort, Pennsylvania
and lives in New York City.

S P U Y T E N   D U Y V I L
Meeting Eyes Bindery
Triton
Lithic Scatter